ANIMALS IN FLIGHT

STEVE JENKINS & ROBIN PAGE

Clarion Books
An Imprint of HarperCollins*Publishers*
Boston   New York

Imagine being able to fly! Soaring, swooping, diving, or hovering—so many animals are able to do what we can only dream about. How do they do it? When, and why, did they take to the air?

The barn swallow, a fast and graceful flyer, spends up to eighteen hours a day in the air.

Insects were the first flying animals.

How did insects begin to fly? No one knows for sure. Some insects may have had flaps on their bodies that they used to warm themselves in the sun. Or they may have started their lives in the water and had fins for swimming. When these insects jumped to avoid danger, some were able to glide to safety with the help of these fins or flaps. After a few million years, most insects had developed real wings, and had spread to all parts of the earth. One of these insects, the ancient cockroach, was one and a half feet long.

The ancient dragonfly lived almost 350 million years ago. Larger than any insect alive today, it had wings measuring two and a half feet across.

Then, about 250 million years ago, small dinosaurs began to fly.

The first flying reptiles were small animals that were related to dinosaurs and lived in trees. Eventually, some of them became quite large. The pteranodon, which lived 175 million years ago, had a seventeen-foot wingspan.

Archaeopteryx, which lived 150 million years ago, was the first true bird. It had feathered wings and scaly skin, like a reptile's.

The largest of the flying reptiles was Quetzacoatlus. Its wings were forty feet across. The modern-day bald eagle has a wingspan of about seven feet.

Flying helps animals escape danger, find and catch food, and move from place to place.

A robin uses flight to escape danger. It may also fly to catch insects, to reach seeds or fruit that other animals can't get to, or to find a safe spot to build a nest for its young.

The barn owl's wings are covered with soft feathers that make no sound as the owl swoops down silently on an unsuspecting mouse.

Different animals have different kinds of wings, but they all work by creating lift.

Reptile wing

Insect wing

Bird wing

Bat wing

Lift is the force that gets an animal up into the air. All wings, animal or man-made, create lift in the same way. The shape of a wing causes the air moving above it to travel faster than the air passing below it. As air moves faster, its pressure is reduced. This results in higher air pressure beneath the wing that pushes upward, lifting the wing (and the flyer) into the air.

The wing of a scarlet macaw

All flying animals, past or present, have wings.

Most insects can fly like a hummingbird. When a housefly wants to land on the ceiling, it hovers right-side up, lifts its front legs until its feet touch the surface, then swings its body around so it is upside down.

Animals use their wings in different ways. Some can hover...

The hummingbird is the only bird that can hover, or fly in place. Hummingbirds can also fly up, down, sideways, and backwards.

The hummingbird's wings can act as helicopter blades, pushing air down or sideways. This is how the hummingbird can fly in any direction.

...others can dive, soar, or turn loops in the air.

Ducks often travel in a V formation. Except for the leader, each duck is partially pulled along by the air currents created by the bird it flies behind. It takes more work to fly at the front of the V, so the ducks take turns leading.

The peregrine falcon, the fastest bird of all, can reach speeds of 175 miles per hour in a dive.

Soaring birds, like the vulture, ride updrafts or rising currents of warm air called thermals. These birds may be able to stay aloft for hours without ever flapping their wings, which are large for their bodies.

Bats have very flexible wings that allow them to change direction quickly. Most bats feed on flying insects, so they have to be acrobatic flyers. They can fly upside down, spin, or turn loops in the air.

Feathers, light and strong, create a large wing surface to push against the air. They also keep the bird warm to conserve energy.

Hollow bones keep the bird's body light.

Strong muscles power wings.

A streamlined body moves easily through the air.

Some birds are unable to fly because they are too heavy or their wings are too small. These birds are able to get around in other ways. The ostrich, which can weigh as much as 300 pounds, can run as fast as a horse. The penguin is a graceful swimmer, and spends most of its time in the water.

Birds use more than just their wings to fly. In fact, their whole bodies are made for flight.

This hawk prepares for a landing.

Insects are the most common flyers. It's believed that there are more than a million different kinds of flying insects.

The honeybee, like most insects, has two pairs of wings.

When a wasp begins to fly, its wings move down and forward like a bird's to create lift. As the wasp raises them for the next stroke, however, they twist upside down. This provides lift on both the upstroke and the downstroke.

When a butterfly is resting, it holds its wings upright and together. When it's ready to take off, it rapidly pulls its wings down and apart. This creates suction that pulls the butterfly straight up into the air.

The ladybug, like all beetles, has a pair of front wings that are hardened into a protective covering. When the ladybug flies, it swings these hardened wings outward and forward and beats its back wings. The front wings don't flap, but they do provide lift once the ladybug is moving.

Bats are the only mammals that can fly.

The vampire bat feeds at night on the blood of other animals.

The bat's wings are supported by four very long fingers. These flexible fingers and the thin skin stretched over them allow the bat to twist its wings into almost any shape, making it possible for the bat to change direction quickly and gracefully.

Most gliders can travel from 50 to 150 feet in the air. The flying fish holds the animal gliding record of one fourth of a mile—more than 1,300 feet.

Flying squirrel

Flying lizard

Flying gecko

Flying fish

Flying snake

The flying frog uses the skin stretched between its toes to glide from tree to tree. Like other gliders, it doesn't have wings and is unable to create enough lift to overcome gravity, so it's not a true flyer.

Flying squirrels, flying fish, and flying frogs can't really fly. They are gliders.

The largest and smallest flyers

The albatross uses its large wings to soar over the ocean for days at a time.

The fairy fly, only 1/125 of an inch long, is the smallest flying insect.

The bumblebee bat, the world's tiniest bat, has a wingspan of six inches and weighs less than a penny.

The bee hummingbird is the smallest bird. Its body is less than three inches long, and its wings measure six inches across.

The largest flying insect is the Queen Alexandra's Birdwing butterfly. It measures twelve and a half inches from wingtip to wingtip.

The Indian flying fox, with wings six feet across, is the largest bat in the world.

The albatross has a wingspan of up to twelve feet, the largest of any bird.

The horsefly can reach speeds of thirty miles per hour or more, making it the fastest insect.

The fastest bat, the big brown bat, can fly at forty miles per hour.

The arctic tern flies a round trip distance of 25,000 miles every year as it migrates from the Arctic to the Antarctic and back.

The spotted whooper swan holds the record for high altitude flying. It's been seen flying 27,000 feet above sea level.

Monarch butterflies migrate from the Great Lakes to Mexico every fall, a distance of over 2,000 miles.

Fastest, farthest, highest: world record flyers

The spine-tailed swift is the fastest bird in level flight (not in a dive). It can reach speeds of 112 miles per hour for short periods.

Inspired by animals, humans have dreamed of flying for centuries.

An early, unsuccessful flying machine.
Unlike birds, human bodies are not made for flight. A man of average weight (150 pounds) would need wings about 140 feet across to fly successfully. Even the strongest man would be unable to flap wings so large.

This helicopter built in the 1800s didn't work, because it is very difficult for a human to generate enough power to lift his body into the air.

The first human flights were made using balloons. In 1903, the Wright brothers piloted the first working airplane. It traveled just 120 feet in its initial flight.

A modern passenger jet flies at speeds of more than 500 miles per hour.

The fastest plane is the SR-71 Blackbird spy plane. It was built by the United States in 1961 and can fly three times the speed of sound (over 2,000 miles per hour).

Common throughout much of the world, the **barn swallow** is usually seen in flight. Its forked tail allows it to maneuver quickly and gracefully in the air, where it feeds on flying insects. The barn swallow, as its name suggests, often makes its home in barns. Its nests can also be found under bridges, in caves, or beneath the eaves of houses. These cup-shaped nests are made of mud mixed with straw, grass, or horsehair and are lined with feathers. The barn swallow rolls mud into balls with its feet and carries them to the nest site in its mouth.

It's smaller than its ancient relative, but otherwise the **dragonfly** hasn't changed much in 350 million years. The modern-day dragonfly is a fierce predator of other flying insects. Butterflies, moths, other dragonflies, and mosquitoes are among its prey. Dragonflies are often seen hovering over ponds and streams, where they lay their eggs. A dragonfly may live six or seven years—a long time for an insect. A large dragonfly can fly over twenty-five miles per hour, making it one of the fastest insects.

The **pteranodon** was a reptile and close relative of the dinosaurs. Pteranodons were the largest and most numerous flying animals for more than 100 million years, before they became extinct about 65 million years ago. The pteranodon had a large brain and good eyesight. It's thought to have hunted like the modern-day pelican, skimming over the water and diving in to catch fish, which were probably an important part of its diet.

In many parts of the United States, the appearance of the first **robin** of the year is one of the traditional signs of spring. These familiar birds migrate to warm parts of the country every winter and return north just as the ground is warming up. They are easily identified by their red breasts and the way they hop around instead of walk. Baby robins are hatched featherless with their eyes closed. When they leave the nest two weeks later, they still can't fly. Their parents lead them to shrubs or small trees, where they learn to climb up and jump back to the ground. After a few days, they are strong enough to begin flying.

The **scarlet macaw**, a large, intelligent bird, is a colorful member of the parrot family. Including its long, brightly colored tail, the scarlet macaw grows to be thirty-six inches long. It lives in Central and South America, feeding on insects, fruit, and nuts. Some macaws live to be more than 100 years old.

With its ability to hover and fly in any direction, the **hummingbird** is the helicopter of the bird world. These small birds (the largest hummingbird weighs less than an ounce) are found only in the western hemisphere. Their long, thin beaks allow them to reach deep into flowers and drink the nectar that is the most important part of their diet. Hummingbirds' wings beat so fast— about eighty times a second—that they look like a blur and make a whirring or humming sound.

Just a few years ago, the **peregrine falcon** was nearly extinct. Use of DDT, an insecticide, was making its eggs fragile, and it was producing few offspring. DDT has since been banned, and the falcons are making a comeback. They live in mountains and on cliffs, and they have even moved into buildings in New York and other large cities, where they hunt and eat pigeons. They catch their prey by making a high-speed dive, called a stoop, and hitting other birds in the air, stunning or killing them.

Like the falcon, the **hawk** is a raptor—a bird of prey. Hawks have excellent eyesight and often hunt from high in the air. They use their strong talons to catch and hold mice, rabbits, birds, snakes, and other small animals and they use their powerful beaks to tear their prey to pieces. Many hawks have become endangered as the woods and fields where they live are destroyed by growing towns and cities.

The **honeybee** is a social insect. It lives in a hive with thousands of other bees. Each hive has one queen, who lays eggs, and a few hundred drones, who mate with the queen. All the other bees are workers. It is their job to find and bring back to the hive the flower nectar they use to make honey. Honeybees must collect the nectar from about two million flowers to produce one pound of honey.

The **vampire bat** feeds only on blood from warm-blooded animals. This small (three-inch-long) bat feeds at night. It lands near an animal, then walks, hops, or crawls up to its victim. It makes a small cut with its razor-sharp teeth and laps up the blood that seeps out. The animals it feeds on are usually not harmed, but the bats can spread diseases like rabies with their bites. The vampire bat lives in Central and South America.

The **flying frog** is found in the forests of Malaysia and Southeast Asia. It has suction cups on its toes that stick to leaves and bark and help it climb trees. When the flying frog wants to get to another tree, it jumps and spreads the skin between its toes to make four small parachutes. The flying frog can't really fly, but it can glide as far as forty feet.

The bird with the largest wingspan is the **wandering albatross**, a bird of the open ocean that can fly for thousands of miles without touching land. The albatross nests on rocks and cliffs at the ocean's edge, where it lays one egg a year, always in the same place. It feeds on fish and squid as it flies. Unfortunately, albatrosses often follow fishing boats and try to grab baited hooks as they are thrown into the water. They get caught on the hooks, and are pulled under and drowned. The wandering albatross is now an endangered species.

The **spine-tailed swift** is a skilled flyer. It is agile as well as fast, eating flying insects and drinking as it skims the surface of a pond or stream. This bird is about nine inches long and can be found throughout most of the world. The spine-tailed swift has been officially clocked at 110 miles per hour in level flight, although claims of much higher speeds (more than 200 miles per hour) have been made.

For Jamie, Alec, and Page

Bibliography

Jill Bailey, *Animal Life.*
New York: Oxford University Press, 1994.

Stephen Dalton, *The Miracle of Flight.*
Willowdale, Ontario: Firefly Books, 1999.

George Else (ed.), *Insects and Spiders.*
New York: Time-Life Books, 1997.

Robin Rees, Clifford Bishop (ed.), *The Way Nature Works.*
New York: MacMillan Publishing Company, 1992.

Chandler S. Robbins, Bertel Brunn, and Herbert S. Zim, *Birds of North America.*
New York: Golden press, 1996.

Barbara Taylor, *The Bird Atlas.*
New York: Dorling Kindersley, 1993.

Copyright © 2001 by Steve Jenkins and Robin Page

All rights reserved. No part of this book may be used or reproduced in any manner whatsoever without written permission except in the case of brief quotations embodied in critical articles and reviews. For information, address HarperCollins Publishers, 195 Broadway, New York, NY 10007.

clarionbooks.com

The text of this book is set in Palatino and Frutiger Bold.
The illustrations are cut-paper collage.
Spot illustrations were created in Adobe Illustrator.

Library of Congress Cataloging-in-Publication Data

Jenkins, Steve and Robin Page.
Animals in flight / Steve Jenkins and Robin Page.
p.   cm.
RNF ISBN 0-618-12351-2   PAP ISBN 0-618-54882-3
1. Animal flight—Juvenile literature. [1. Animal flight. 2. Flight.]
I. Jenkins, Steve, 1952– ill. II. Title.
QP310.F5 P34 2001   573.7'98—dc21   2001024103

PAP ISBN-13: 978-0618-54882-8

Printed in China
SCP 22 21 20 19 18 17
4500847036